The Dachshund Lovers Coloring Book

By Mindful Coloring Books

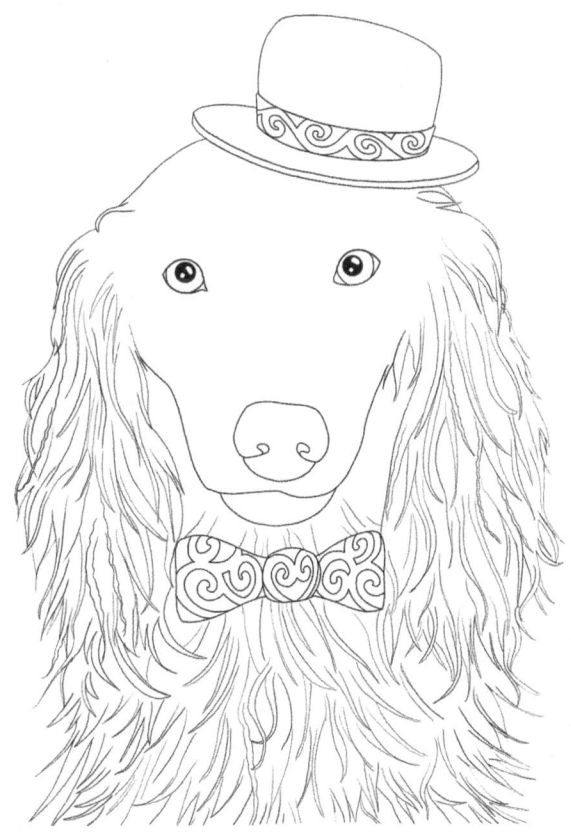

Copyright © 2016 by Mindful Coloring Books

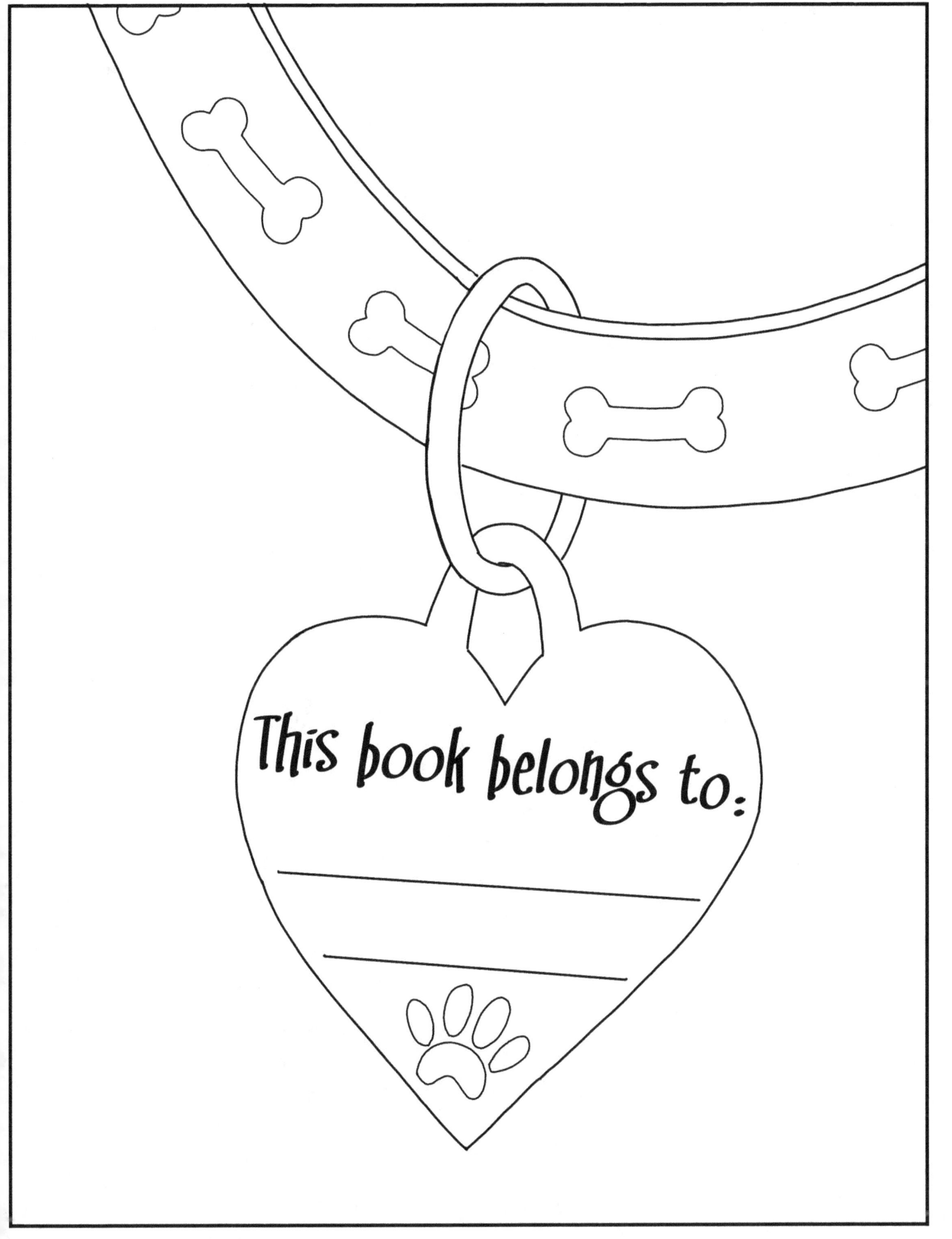

This book belongs to:

_____

_____

Coloring Tips

~ Sometimes what you think the color will look like and what it will actually look like are very different. Use the color test page.

~ Don't press too hard. Start out coloring lightly and you can always go back and make it darker.

~ Keep your pencil tips sharp so you can get into all the intricate spaces.

~ Using markers? Place a scrap piece of paper behind the page you are coloring. Pages in this book are only printed on one side but there is still the risk of bleed through to the next page.

~ Try different coloring utensils marketed for adults. It is fun and quality can vary greatly.

COLOR TEST PAGE

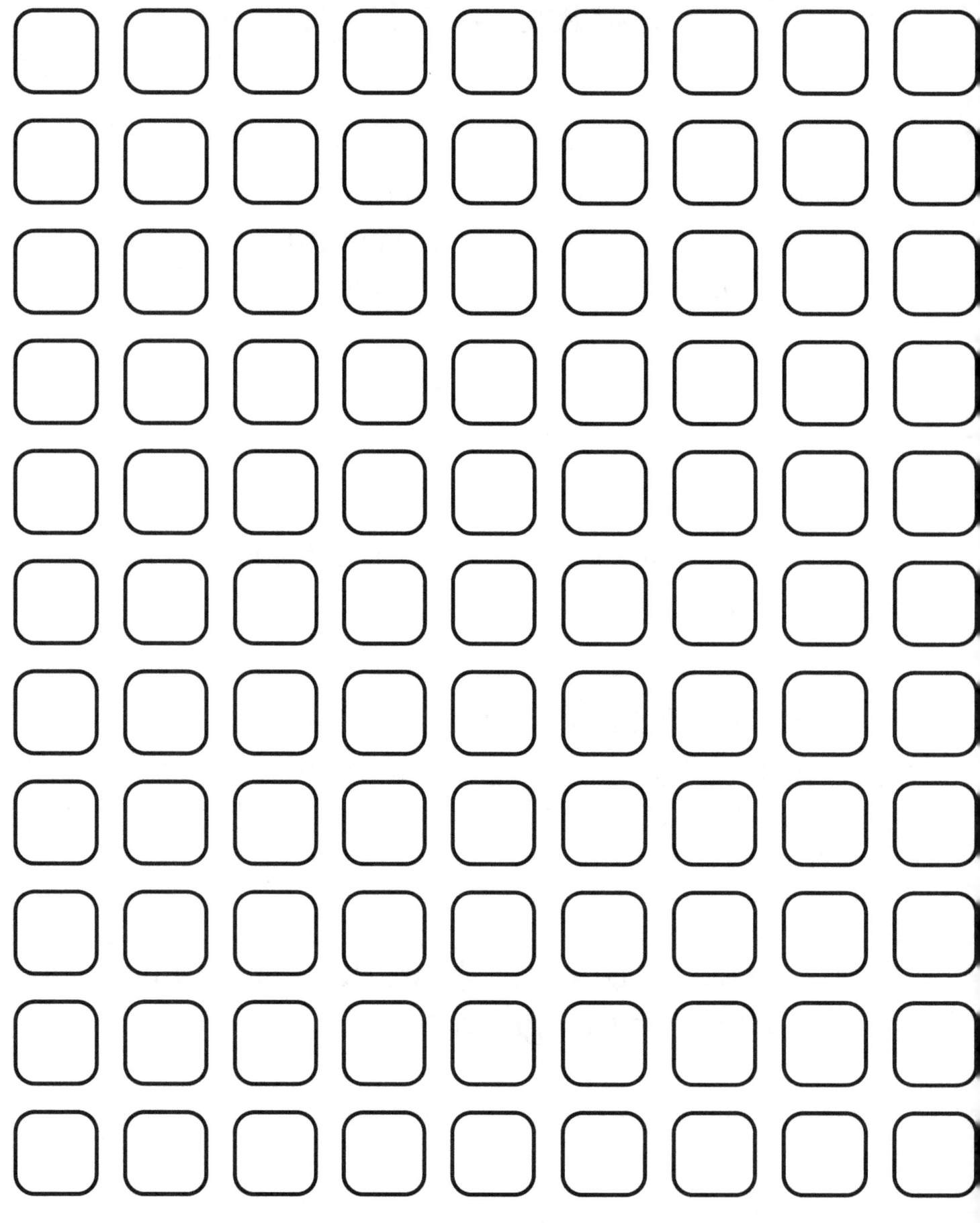

COLOR TEST PAGE

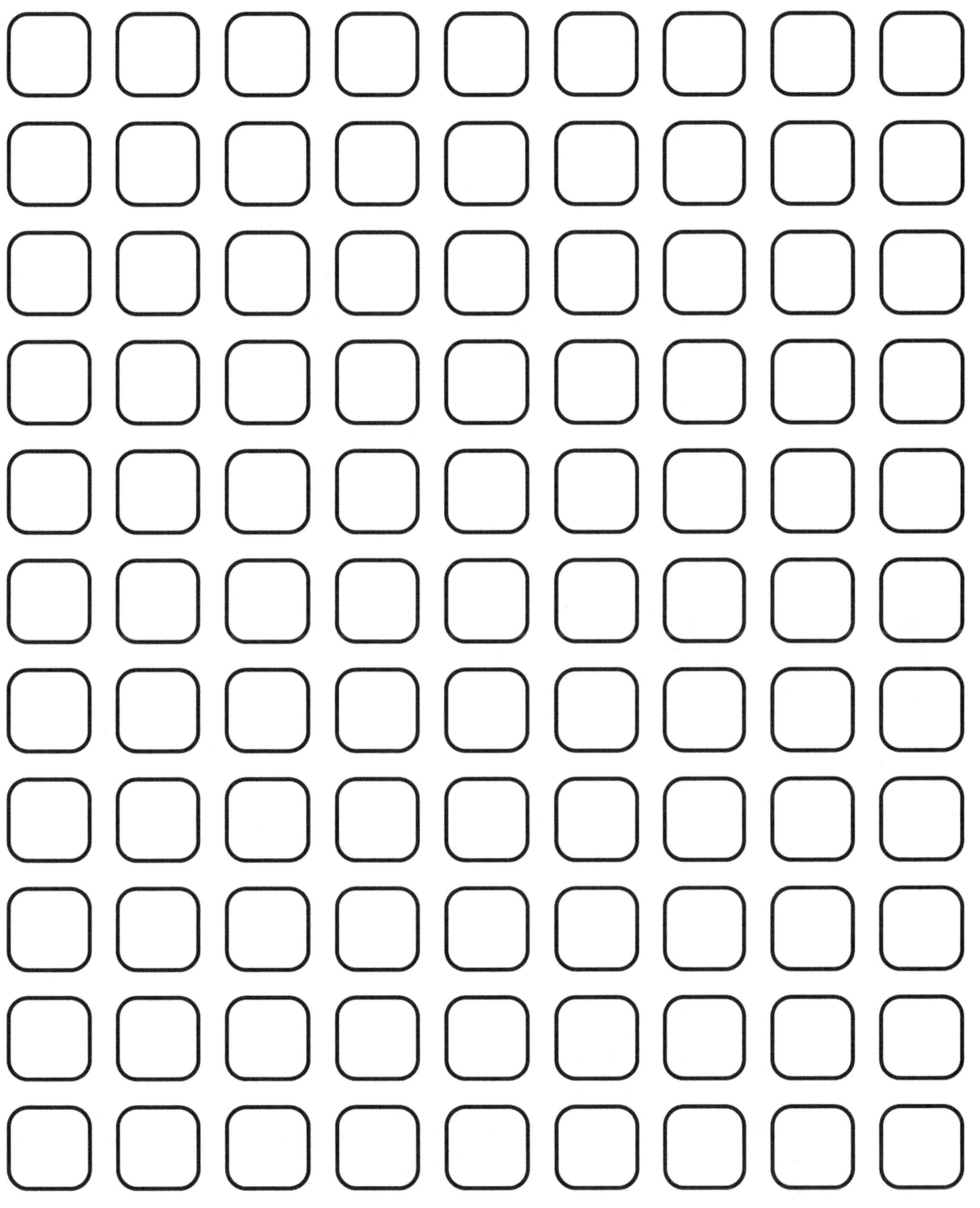

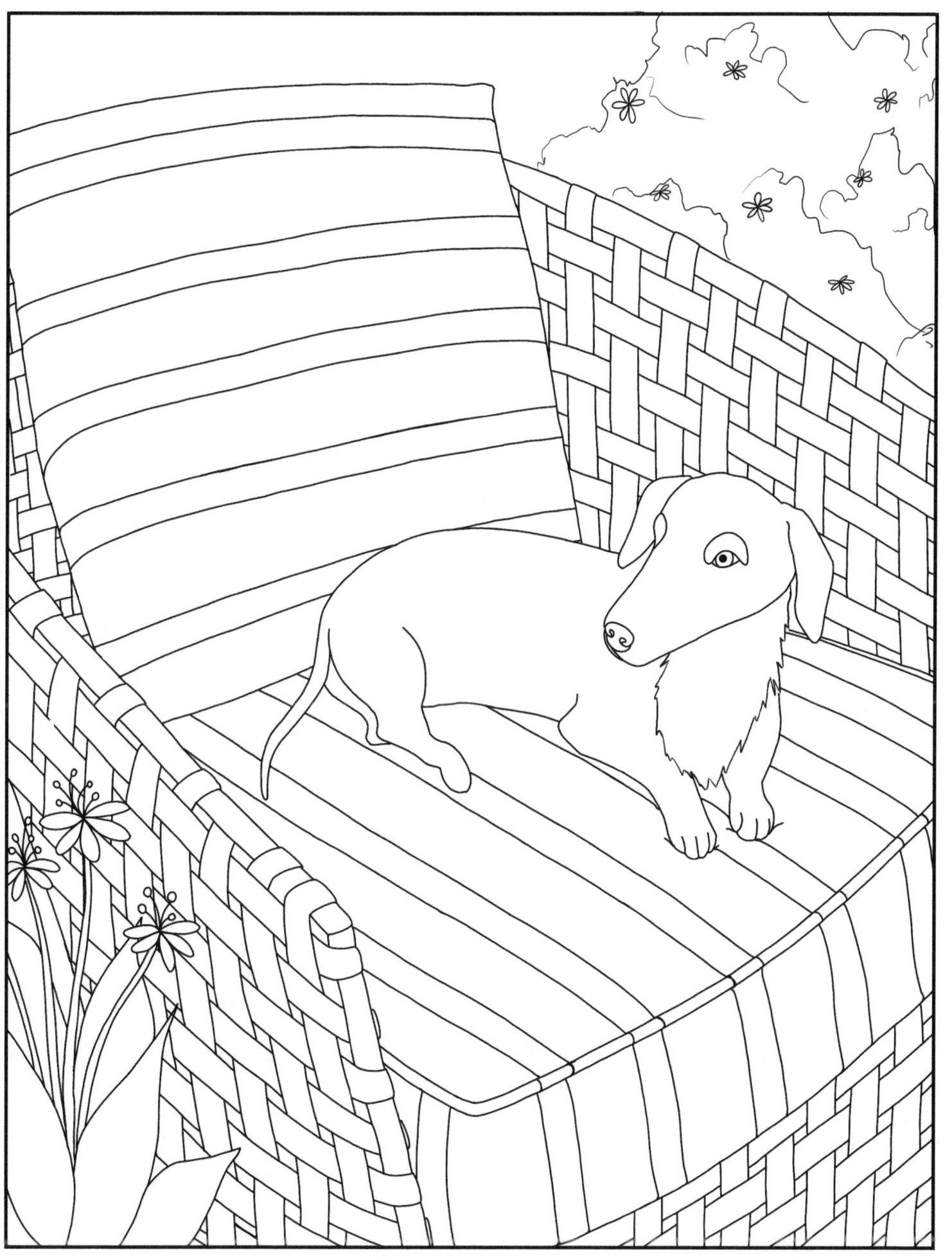

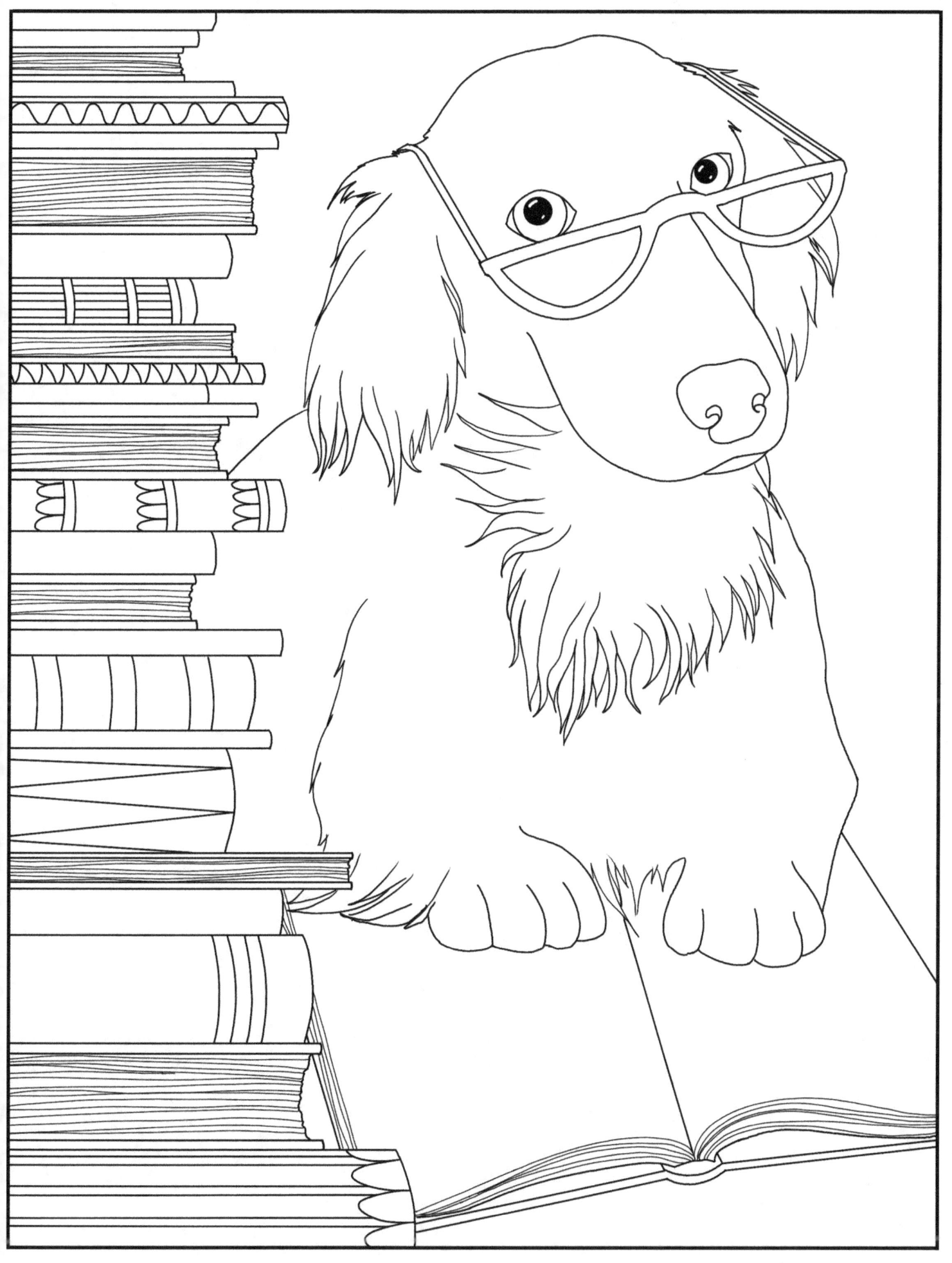

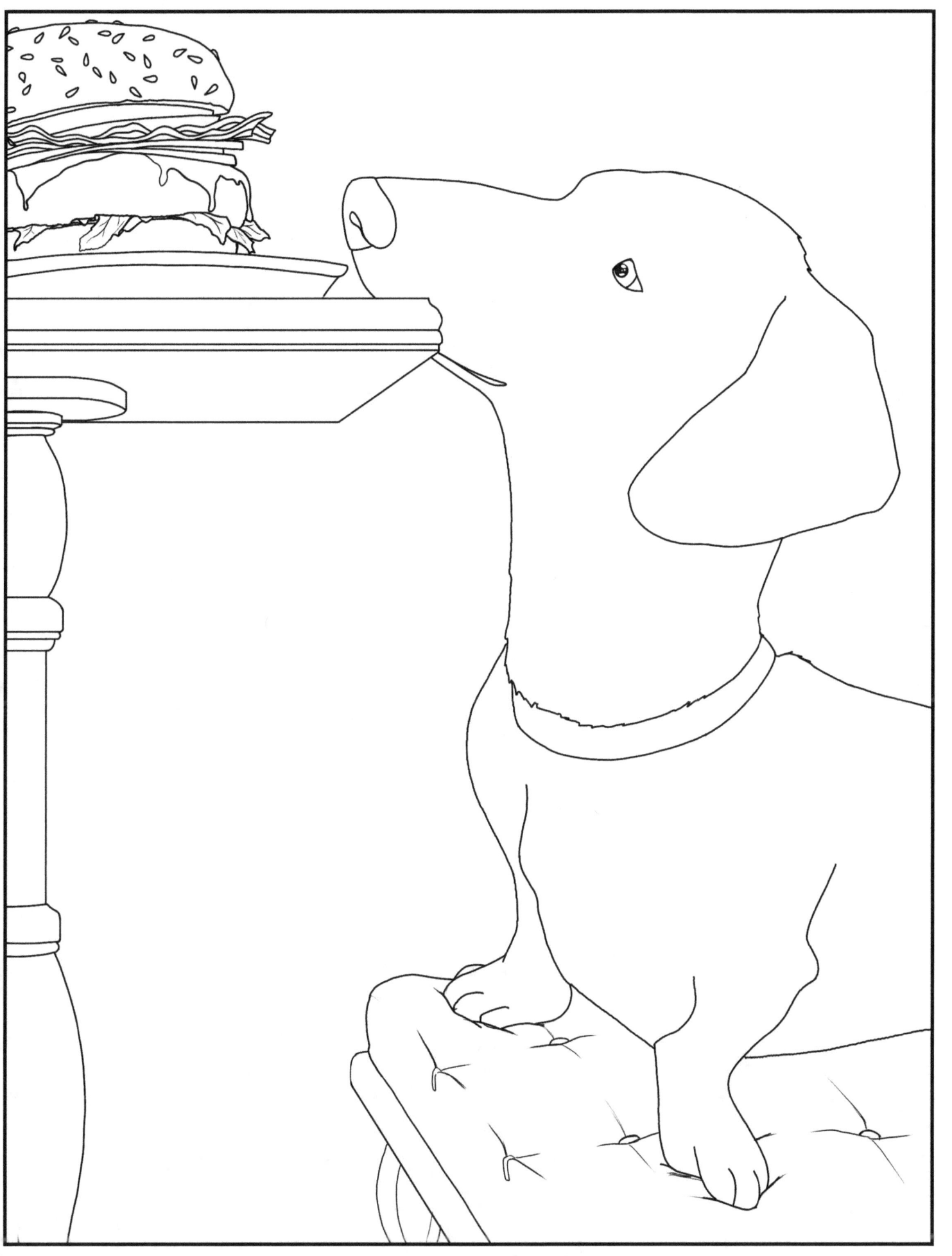

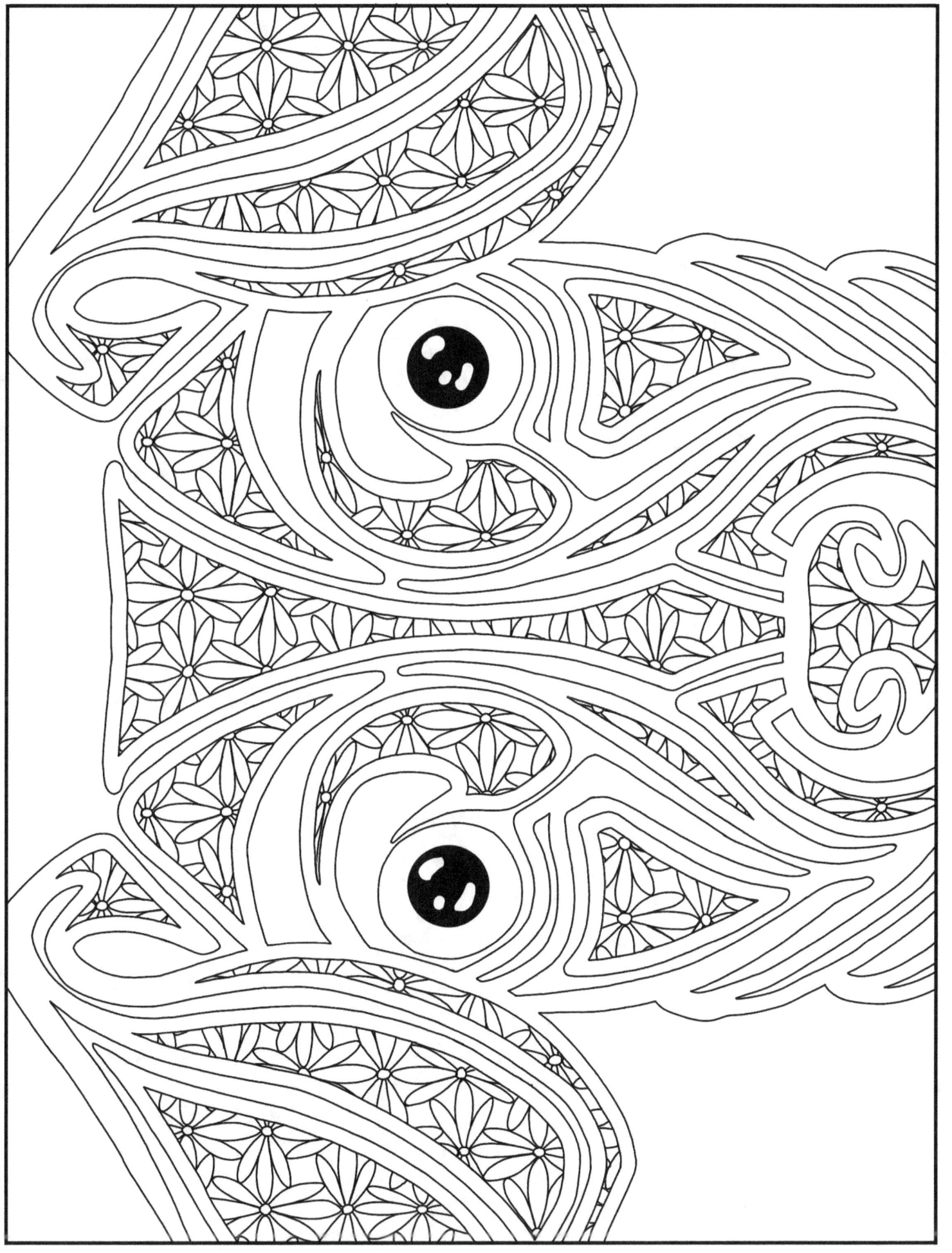

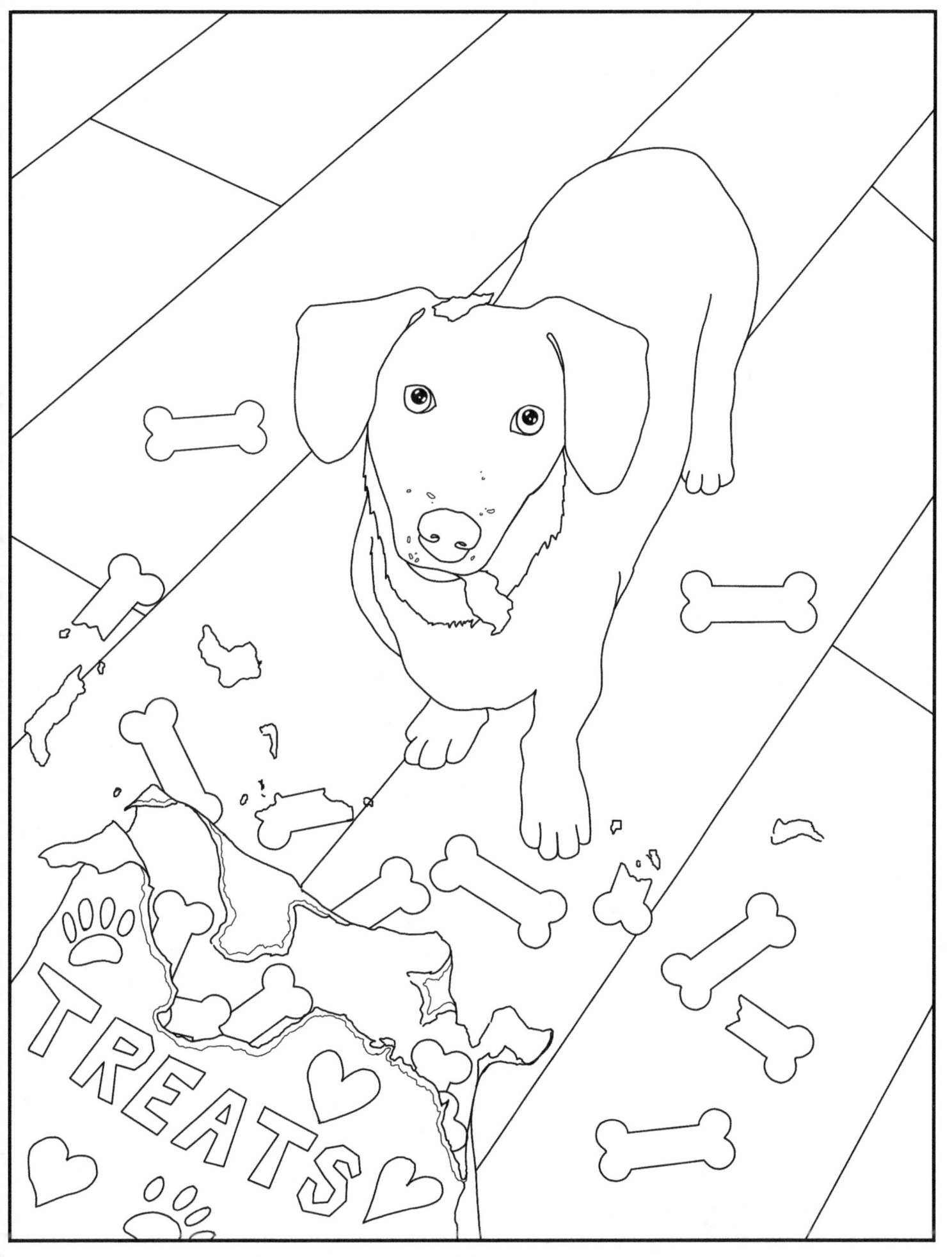

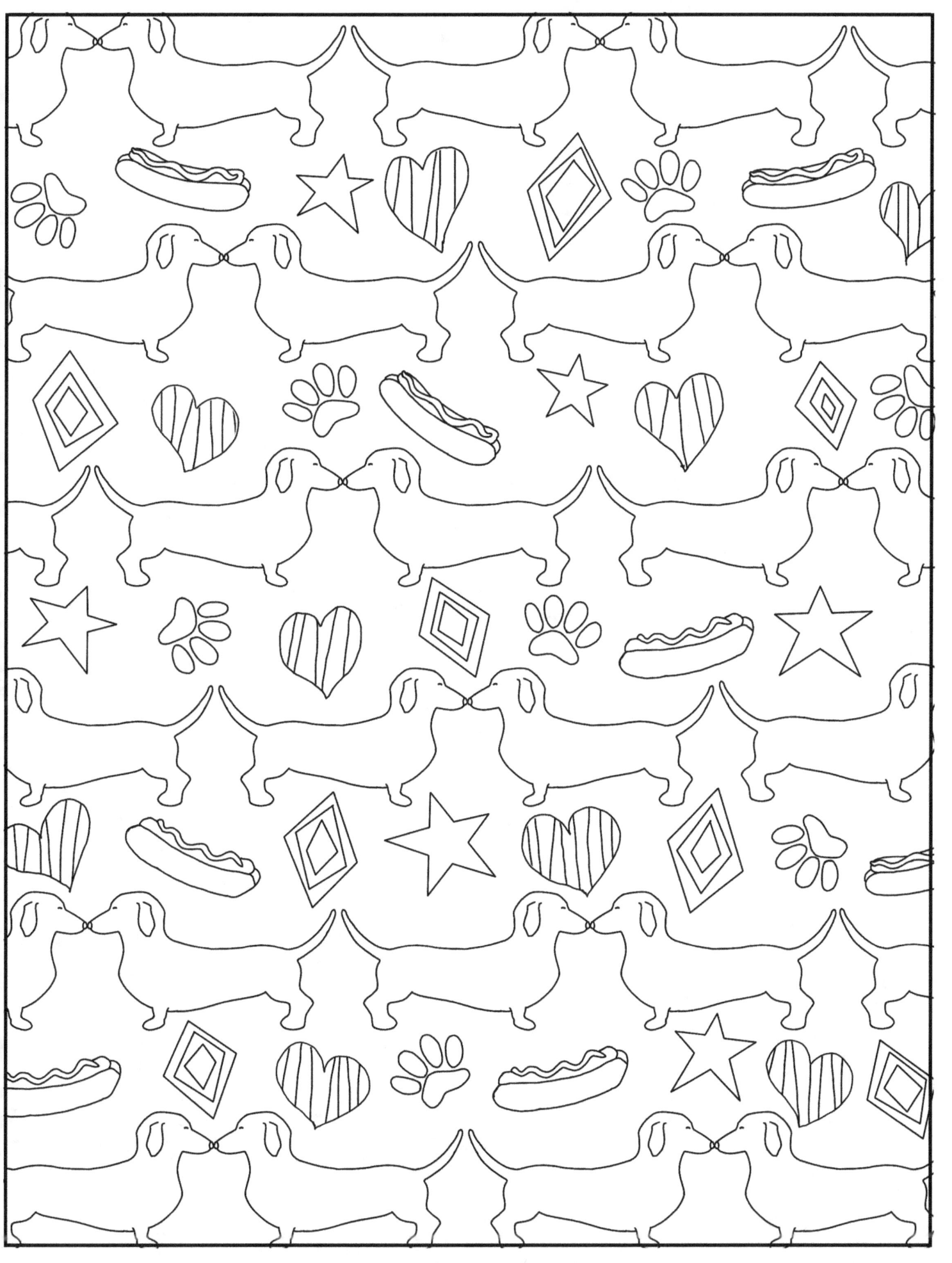

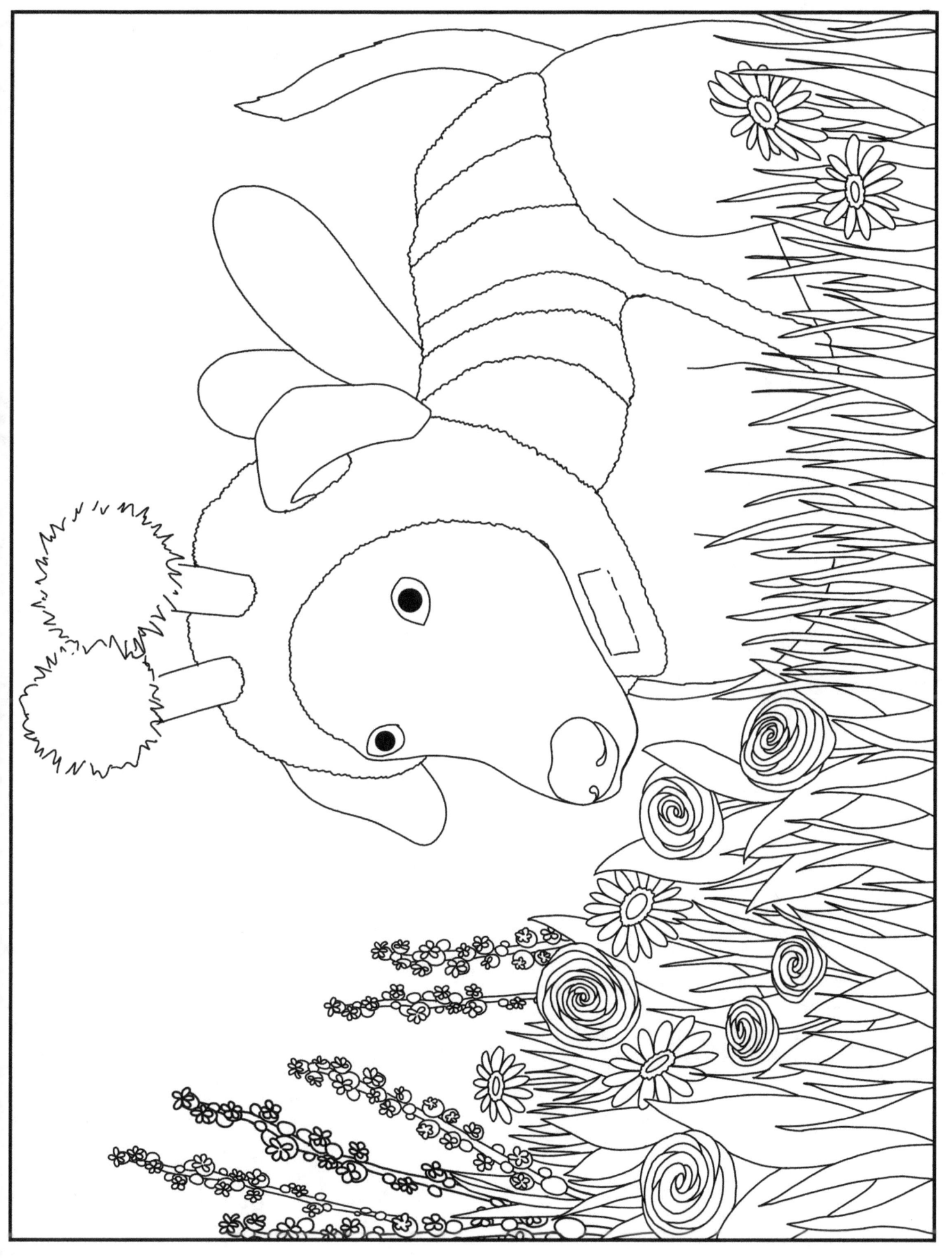

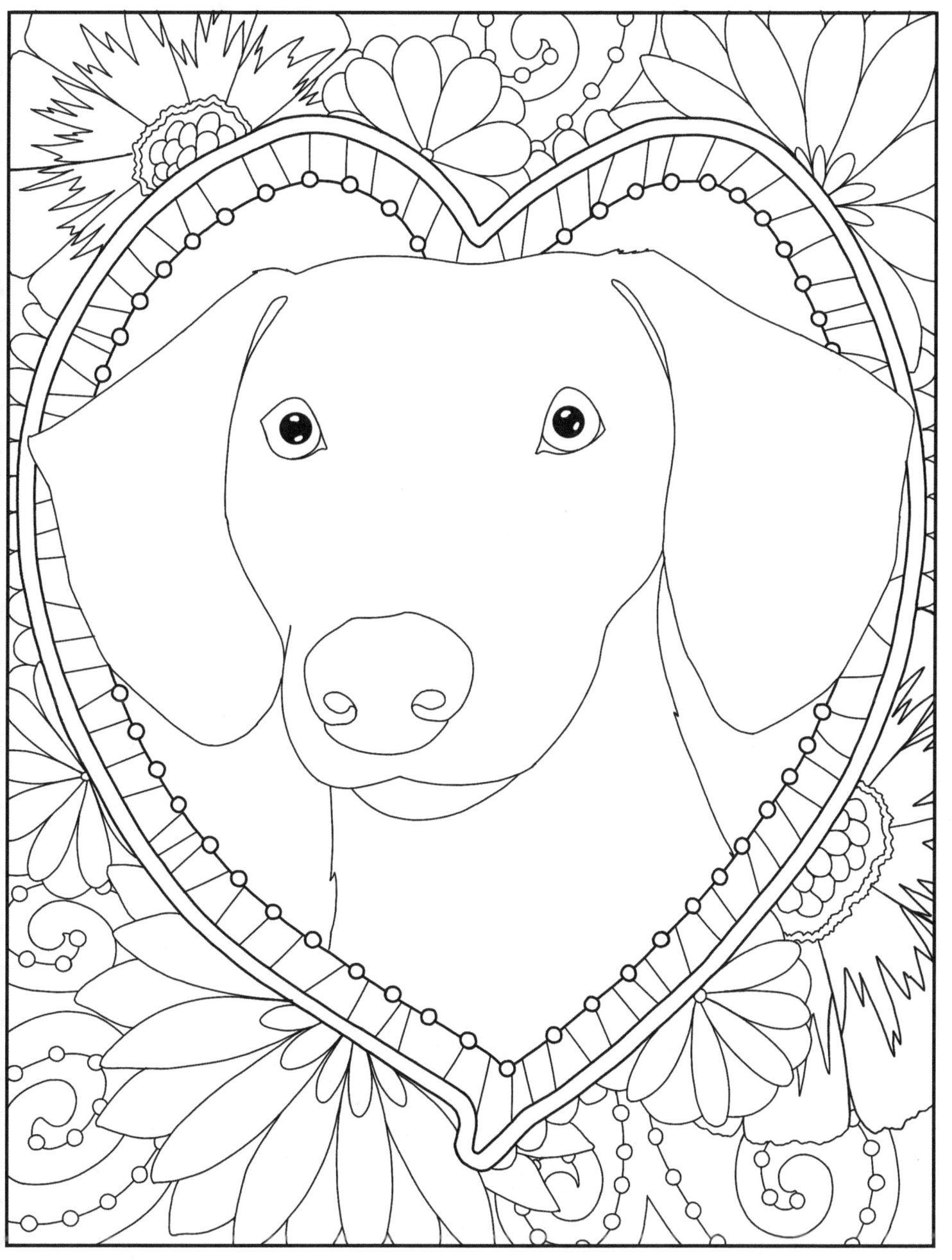

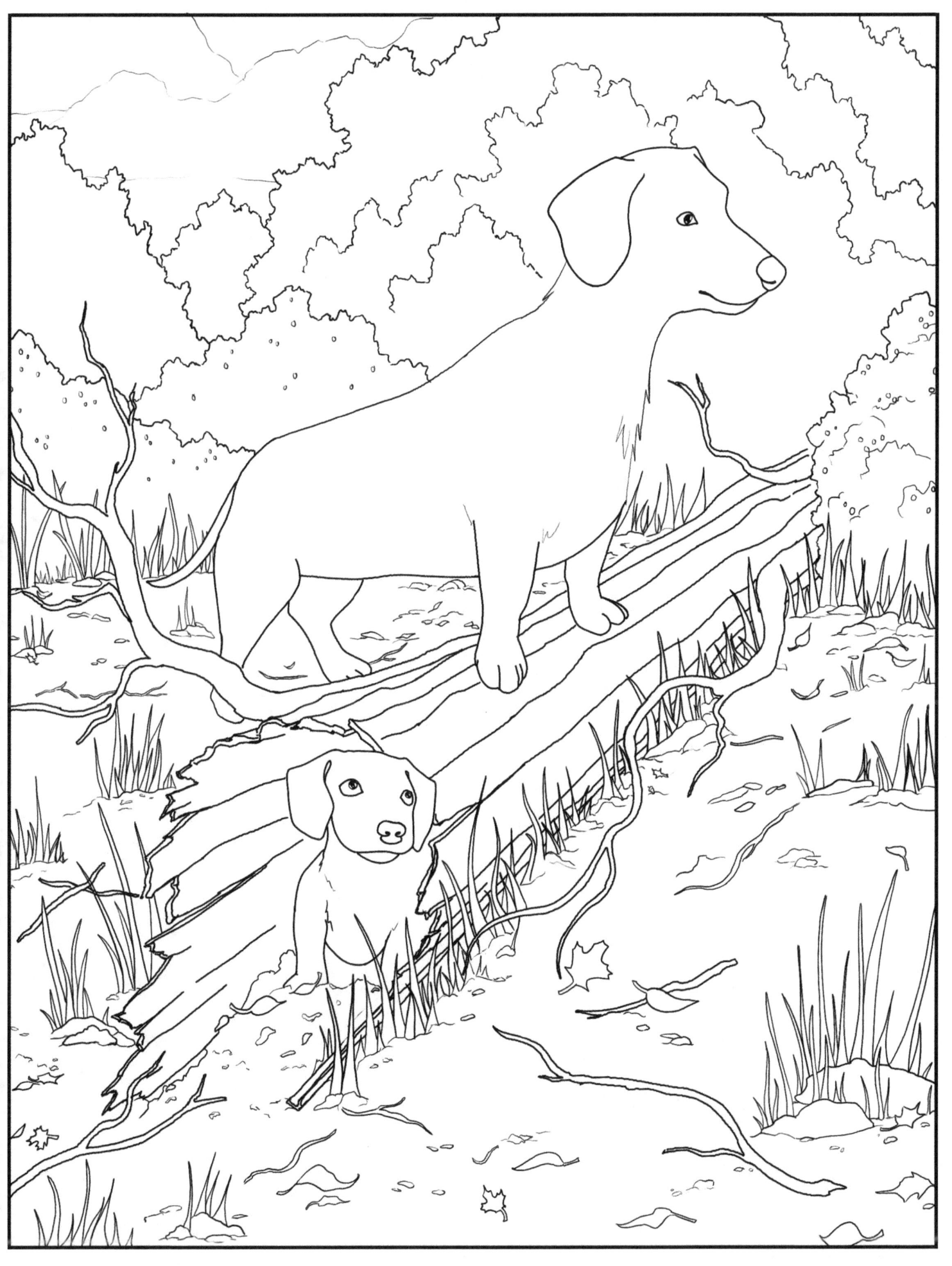

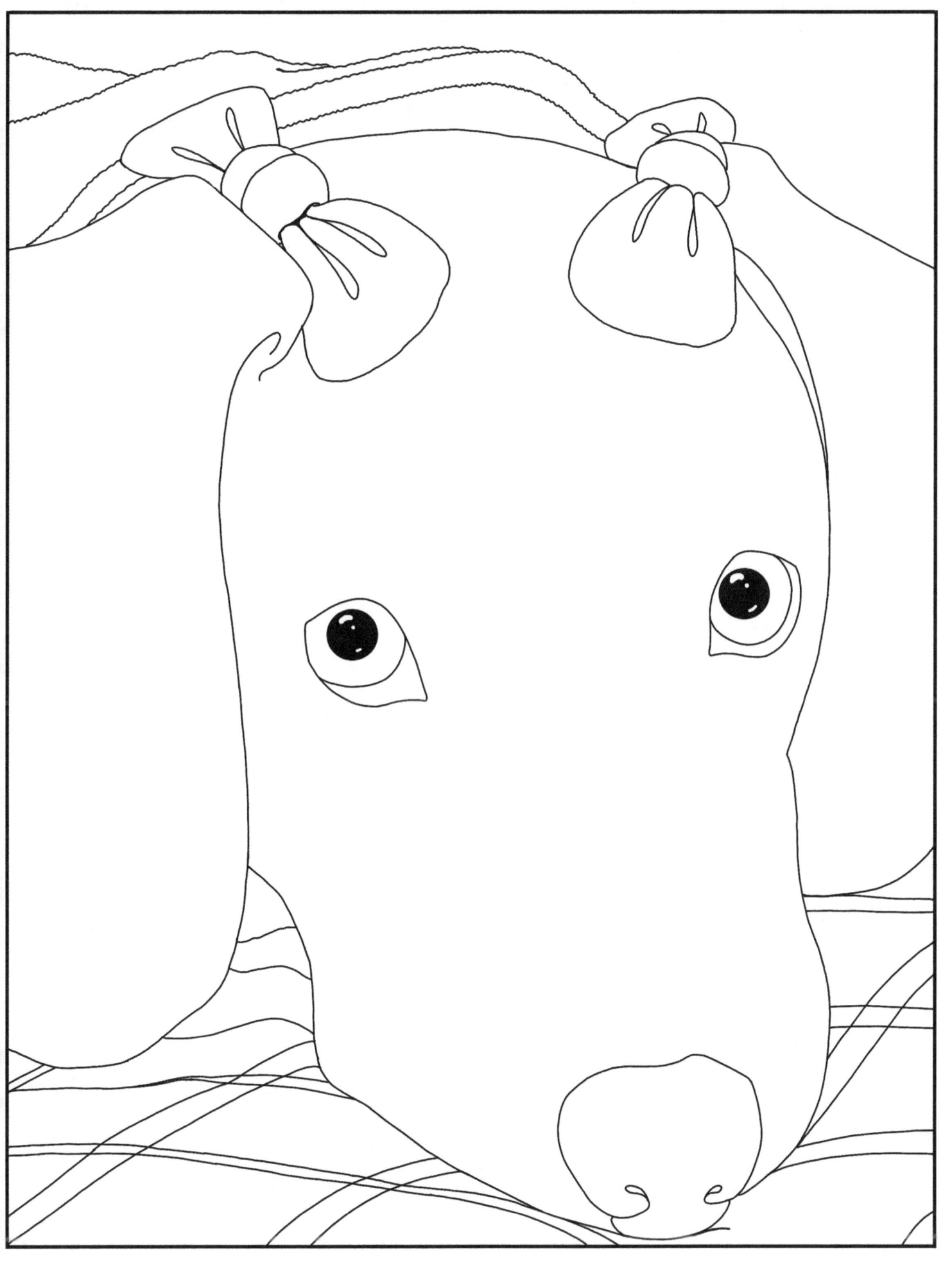

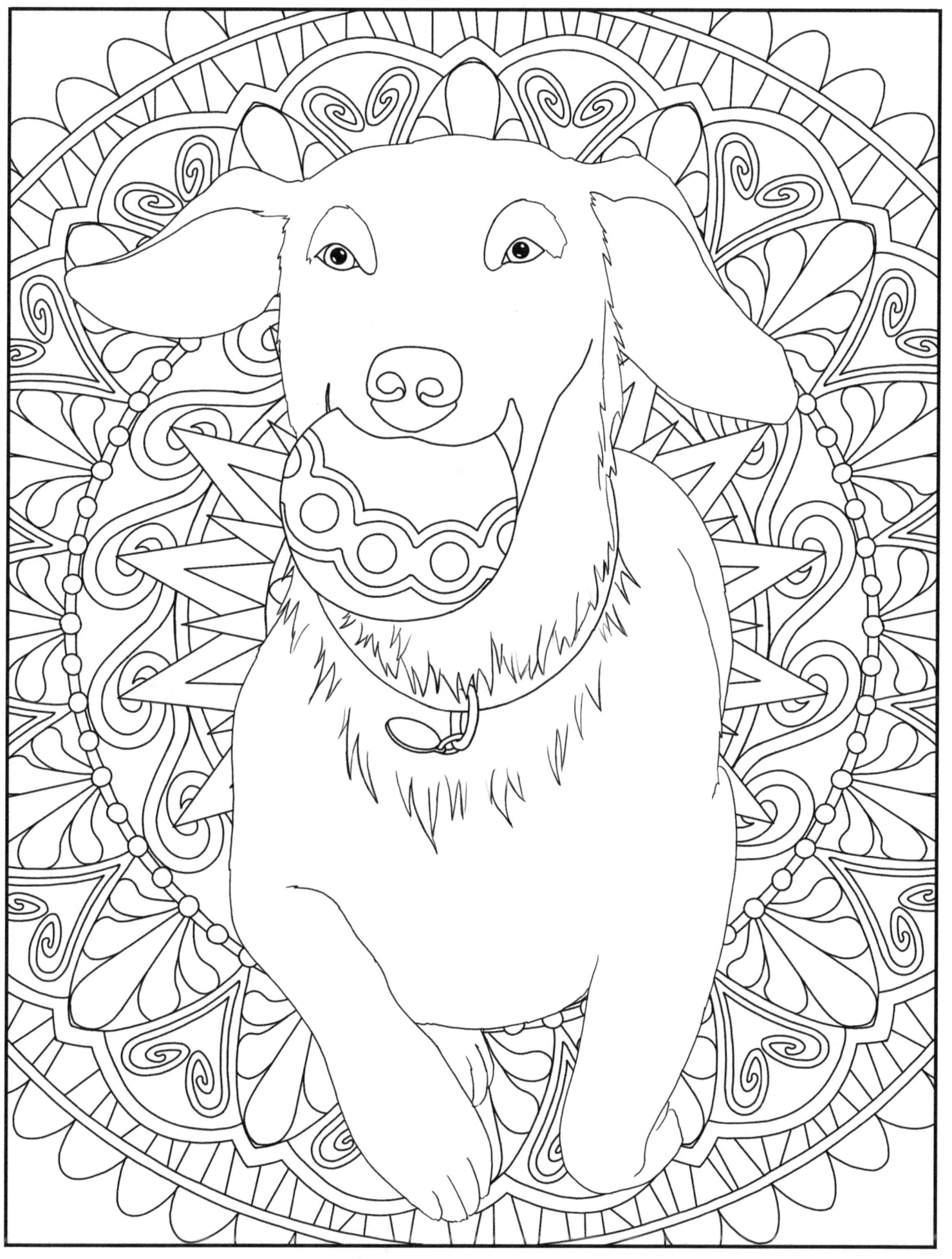

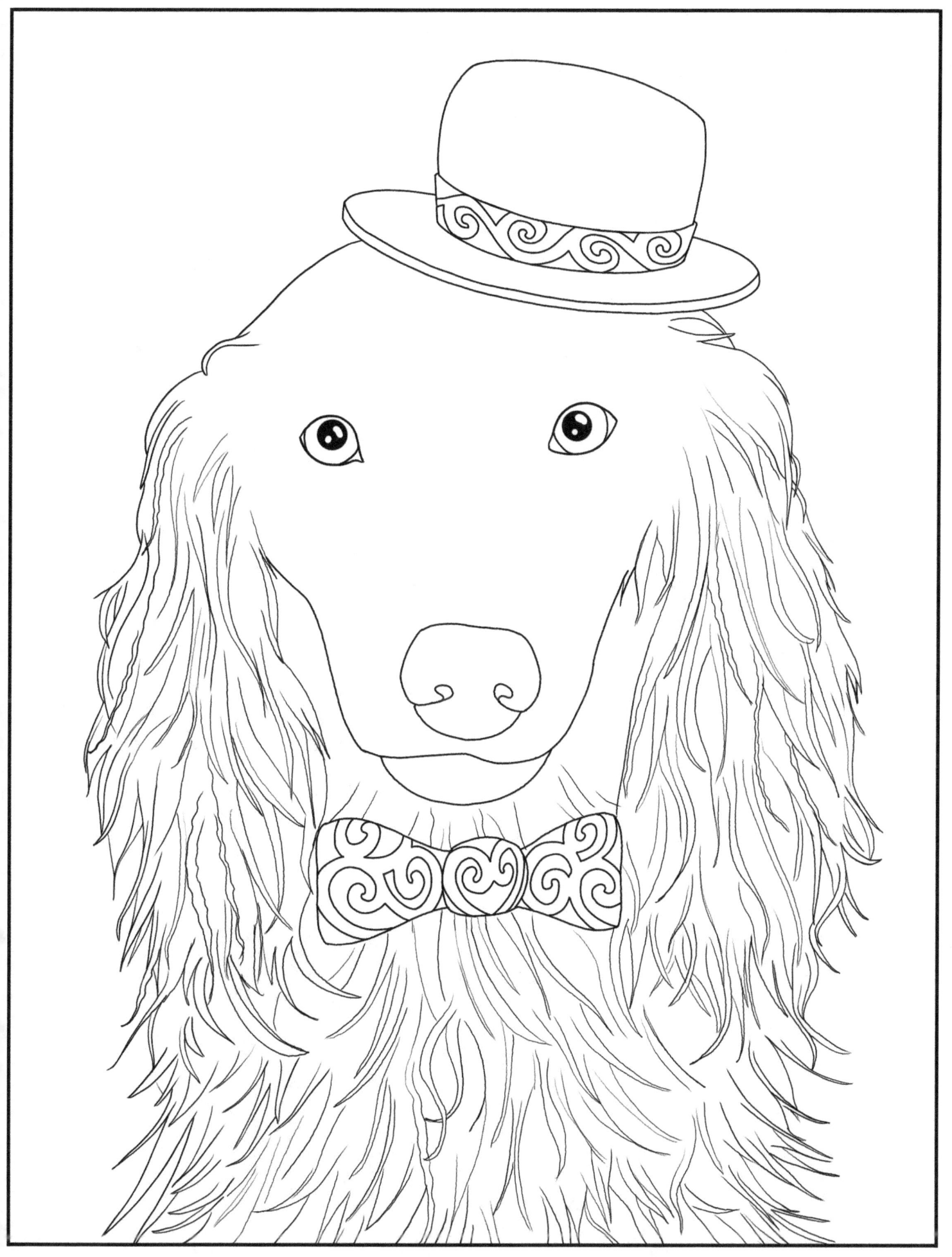

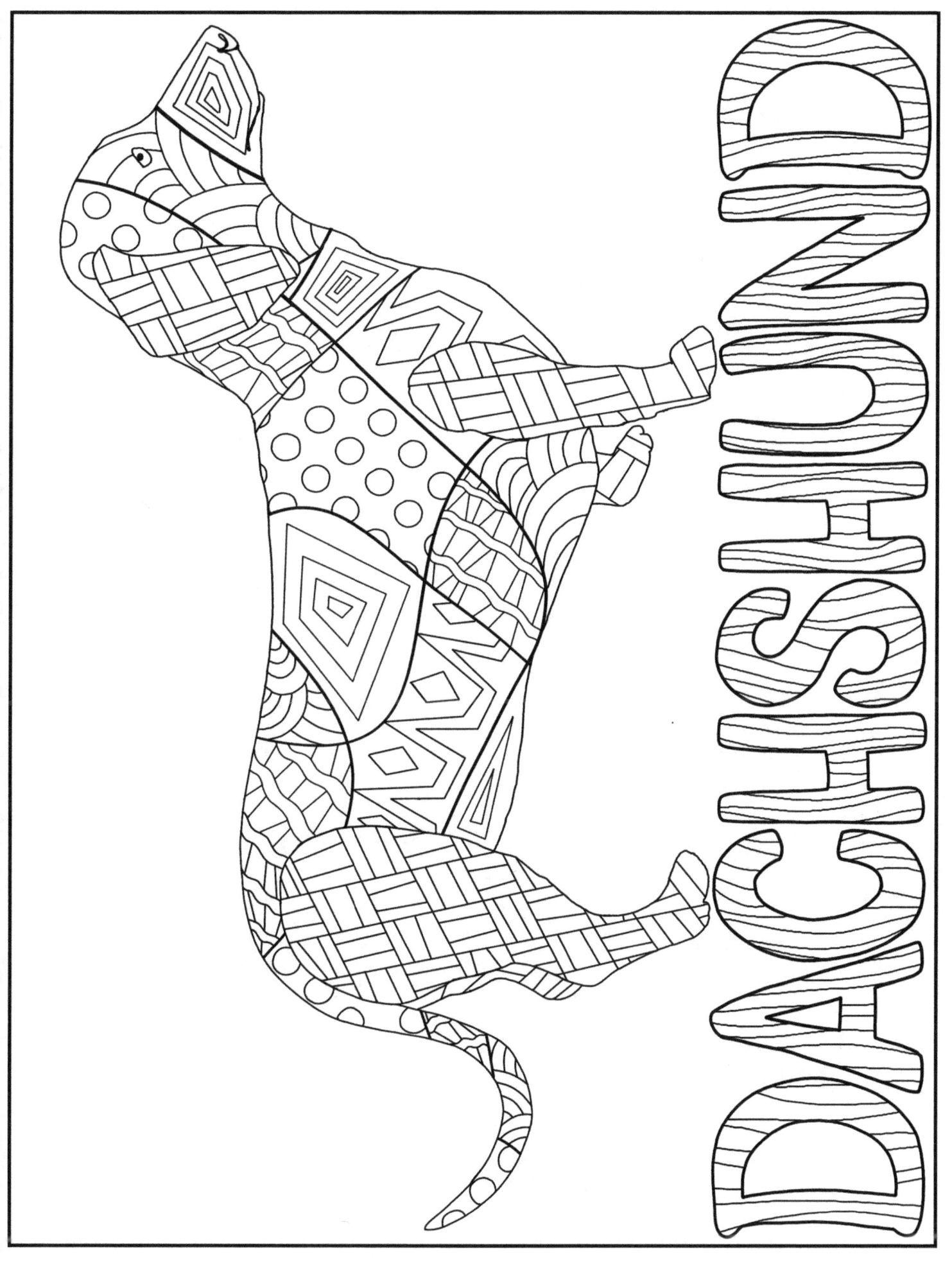

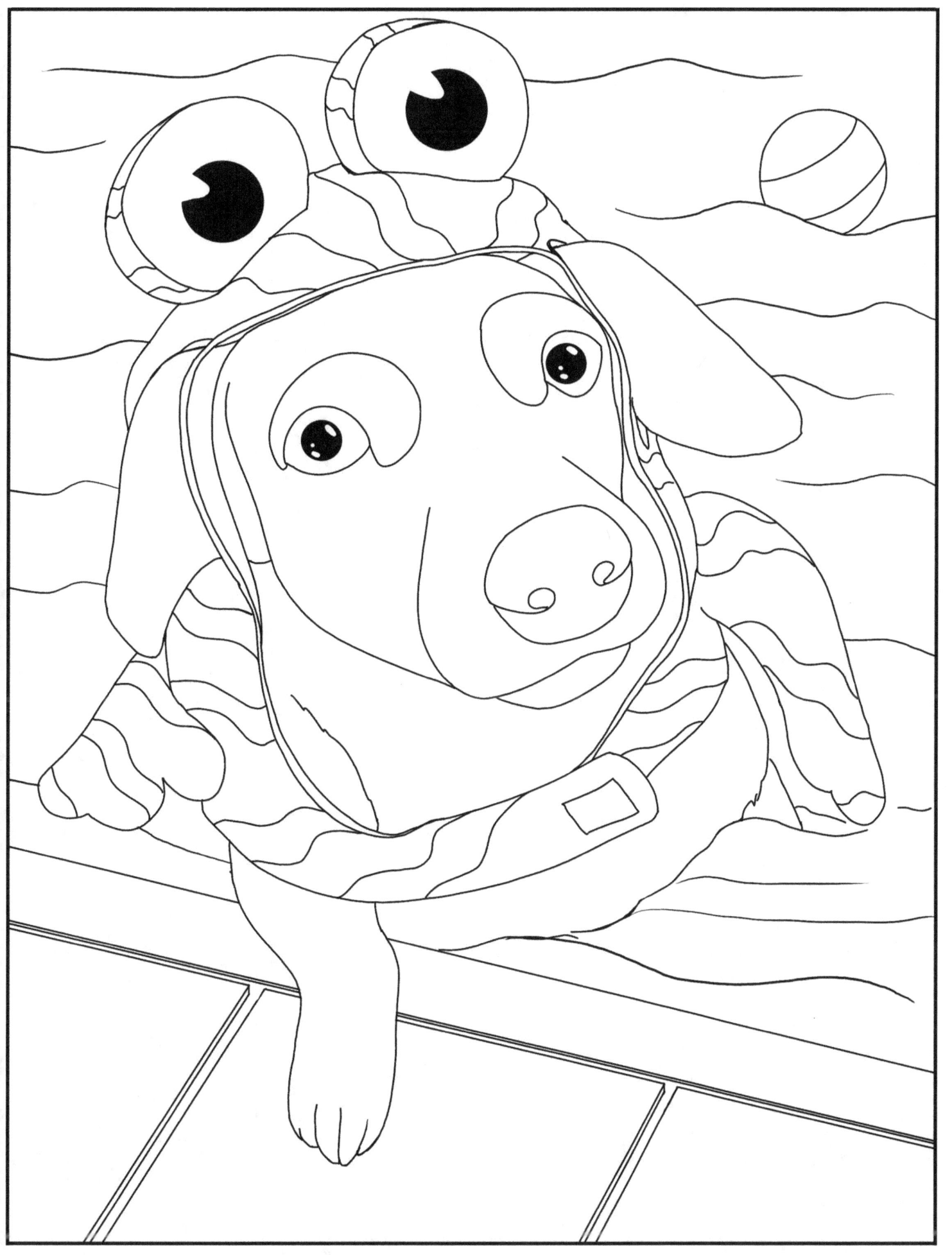

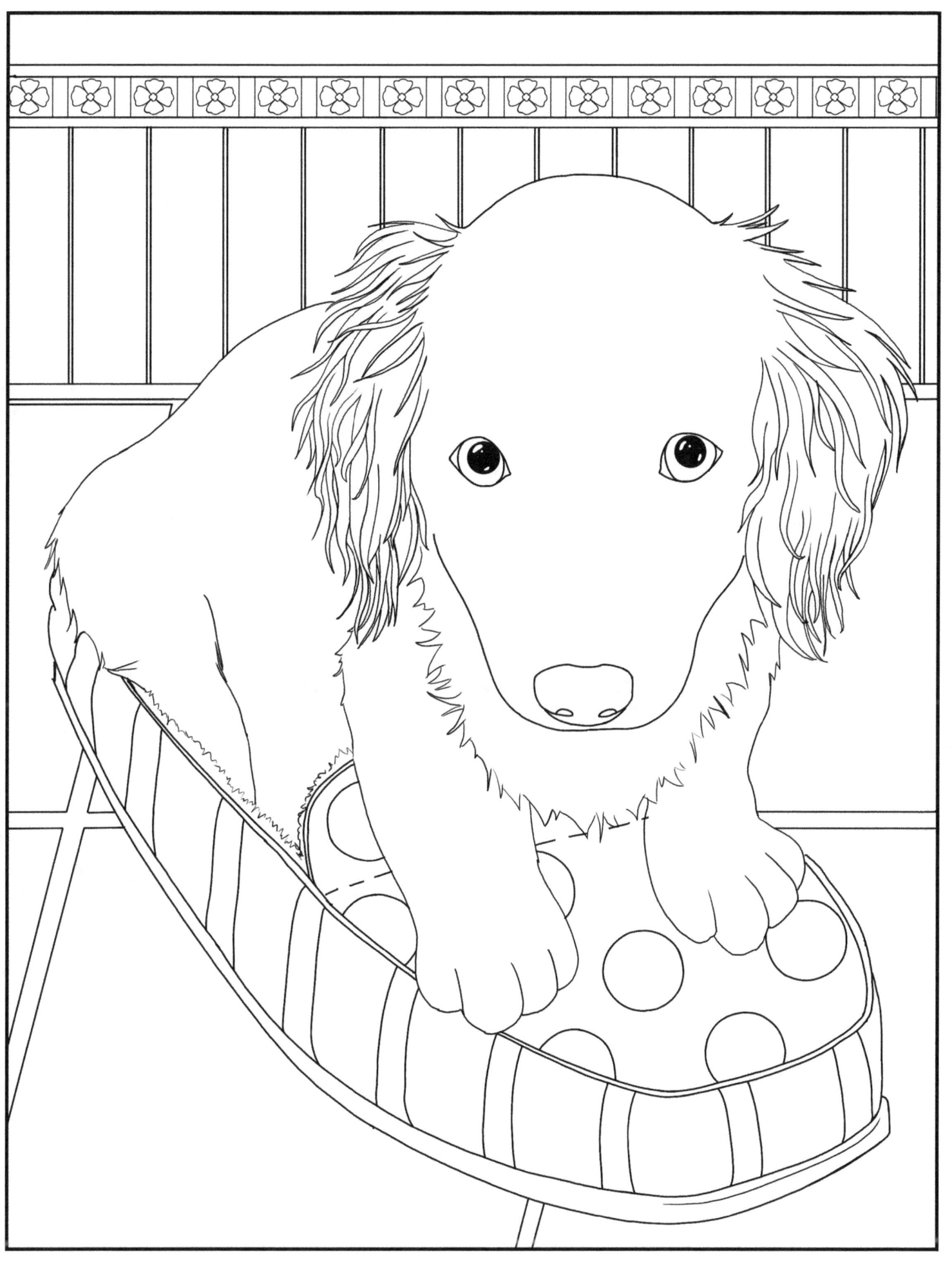

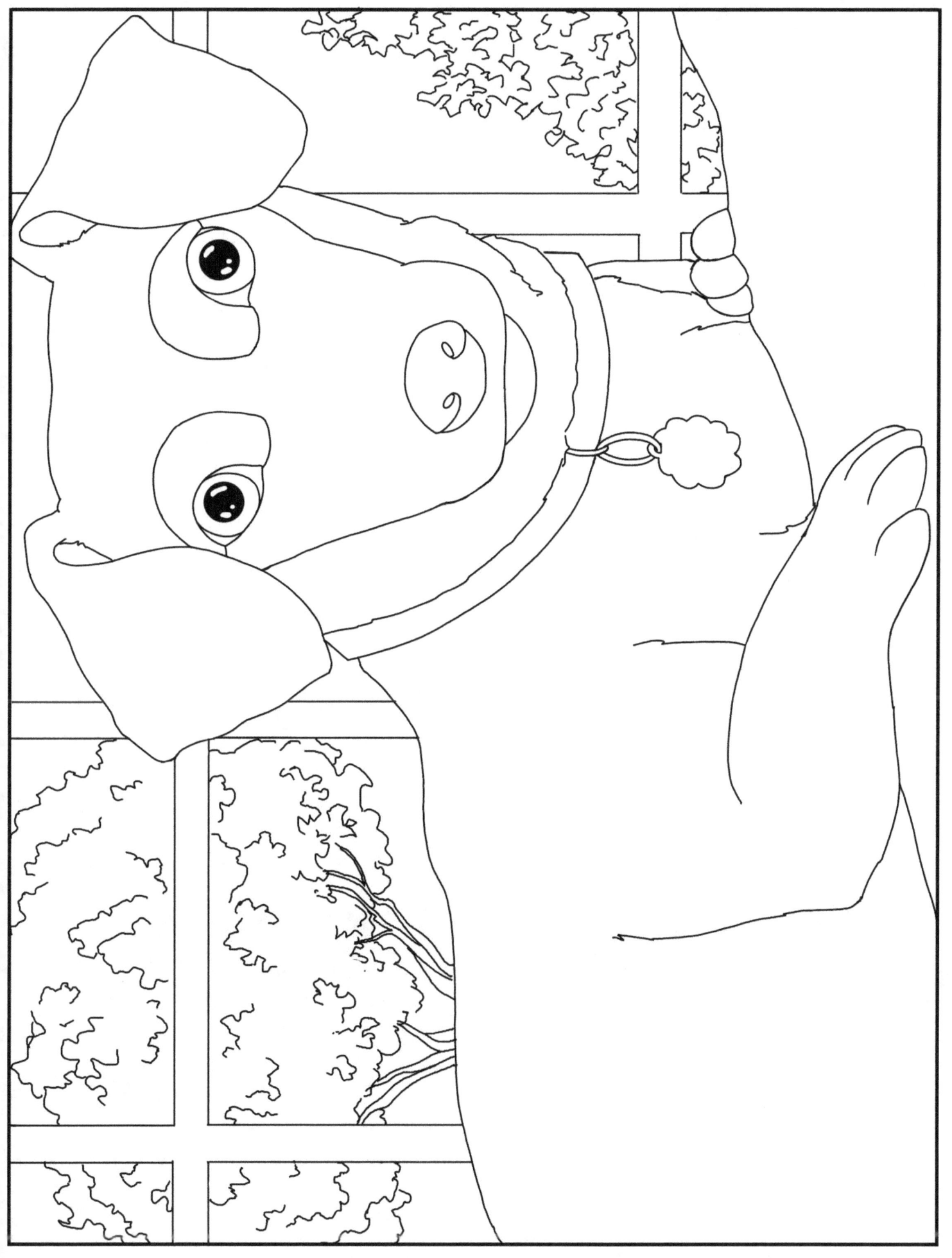

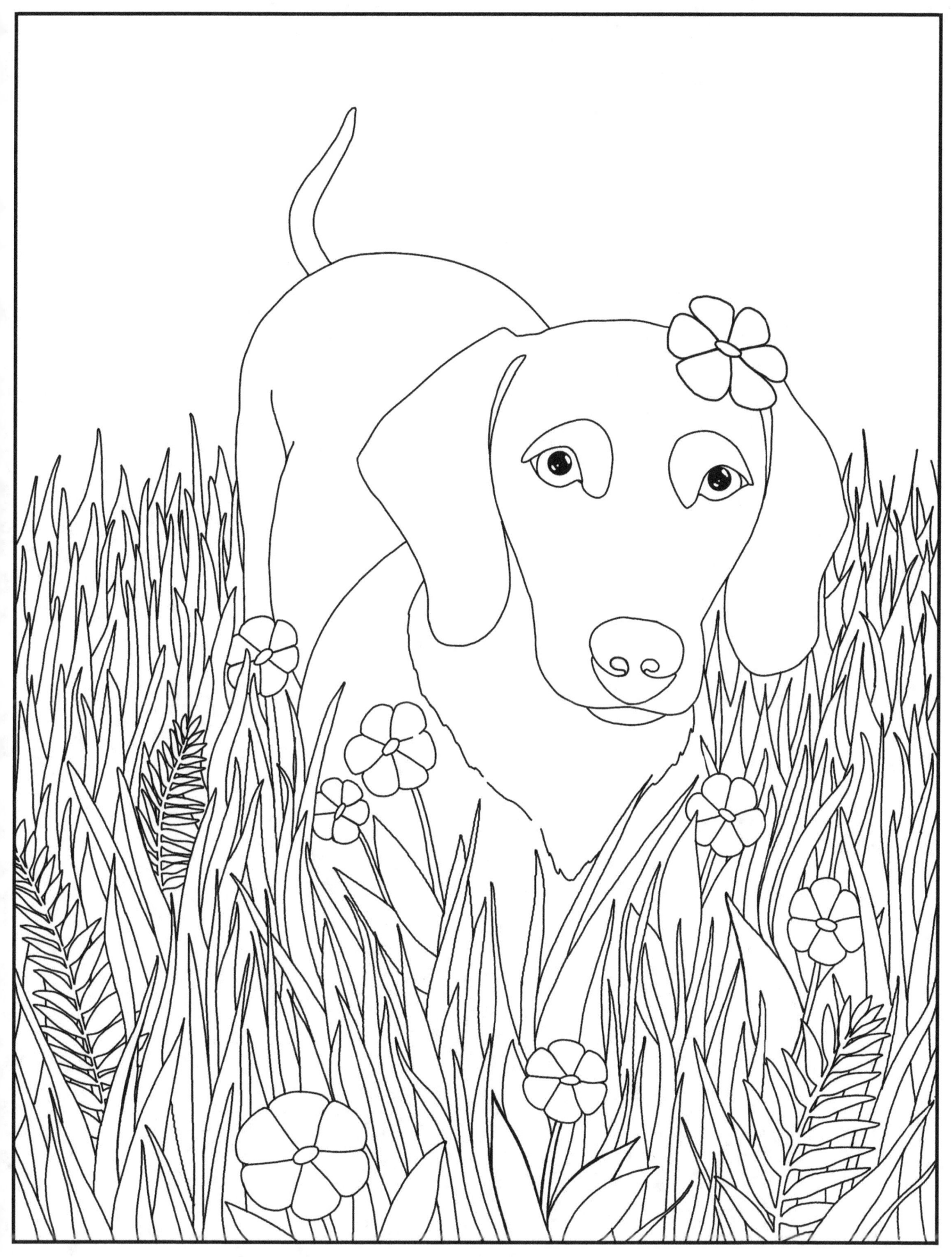

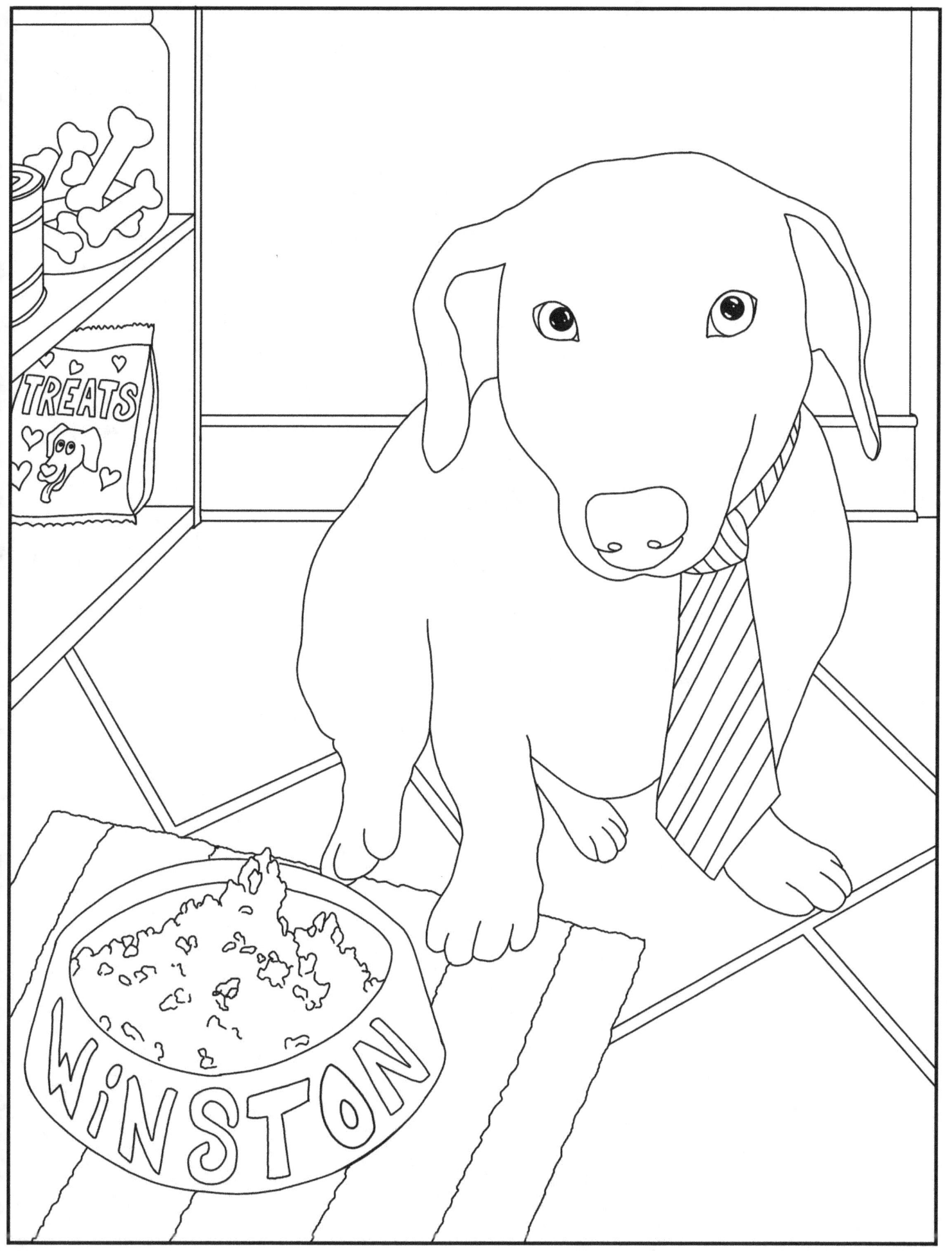

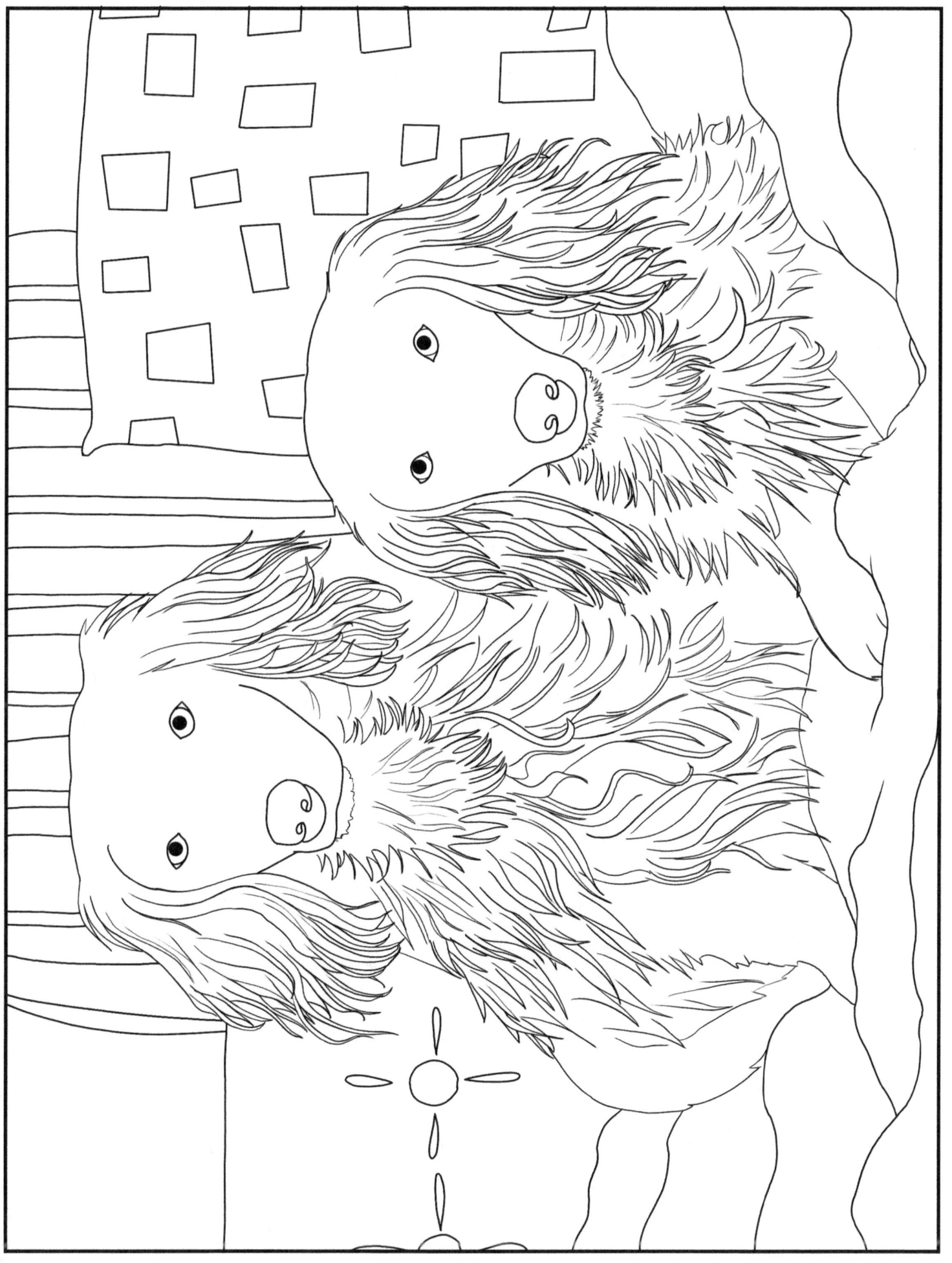

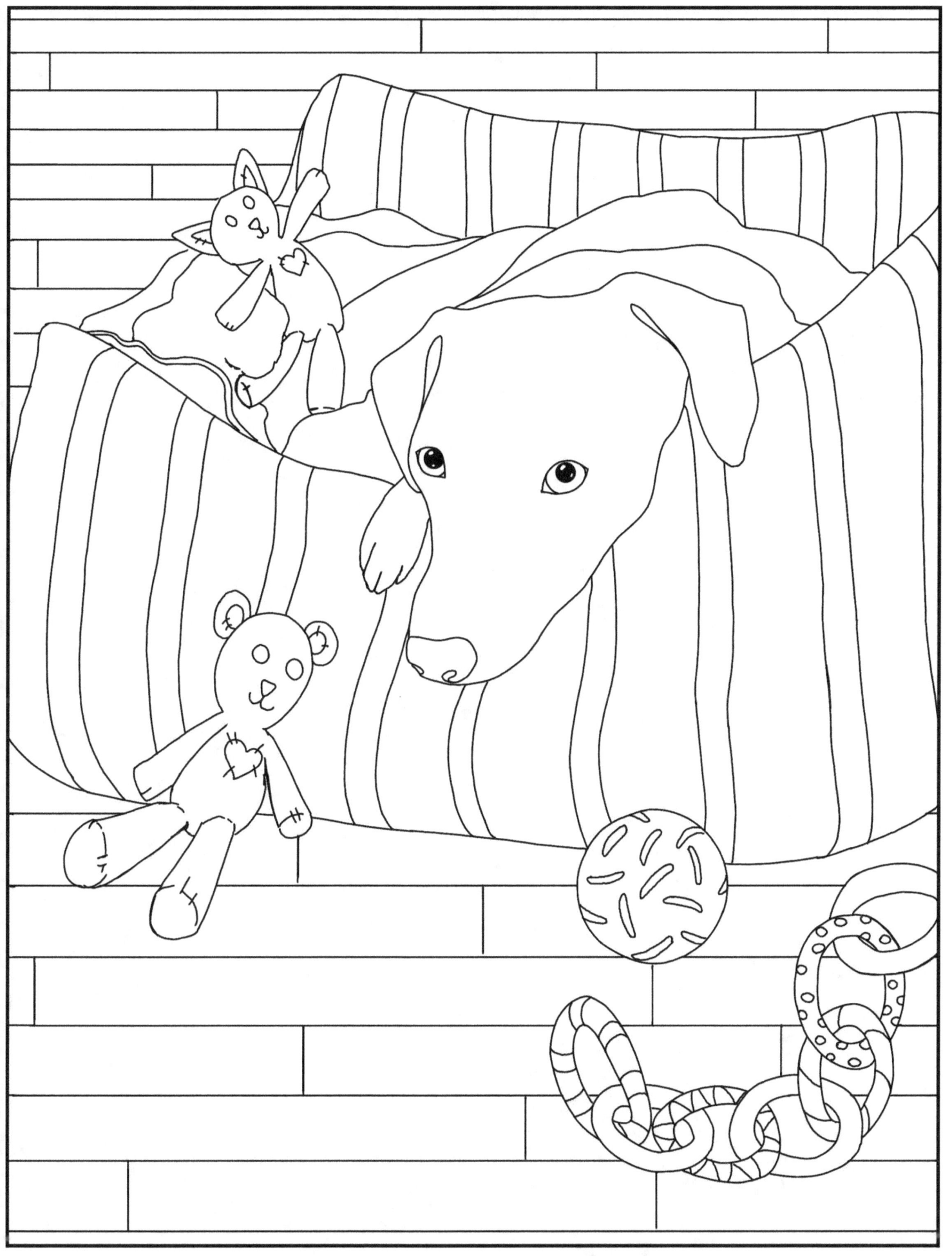

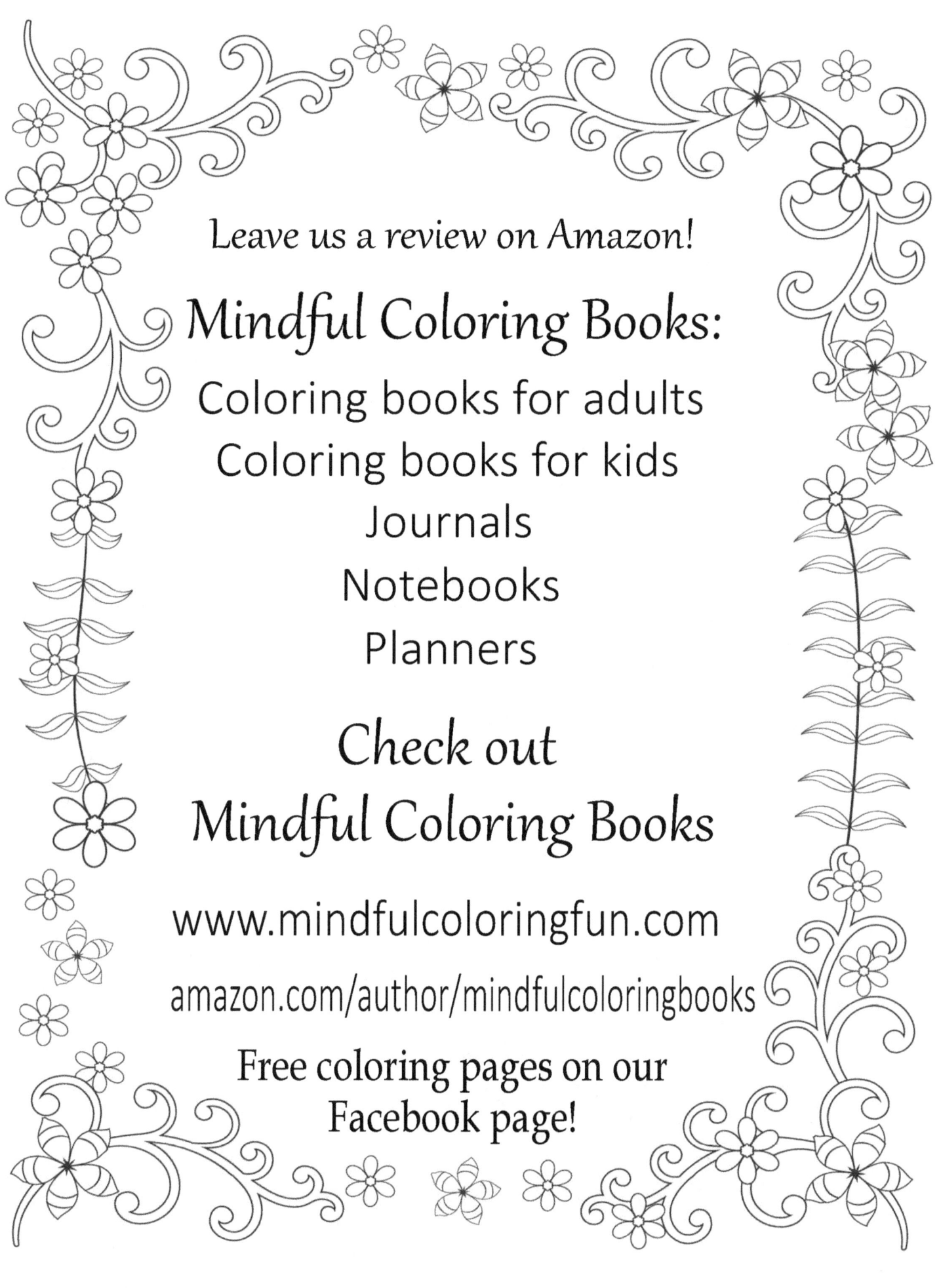

Leave us a review on Amazon!

Mindful Coloring Books:

Coloring books for adults

Coloring books for kids

Journals

Notebooks

Planners

Check out
Mindful Coloring Books

www.mindfulcoloringfun.com

amazon.com/author/mindfulcoloringbooks

Free coloring pages on our
Facebook page!

Enjoy these preview pages from some of our other coloring books!

The Pug Lovers Coloring Book

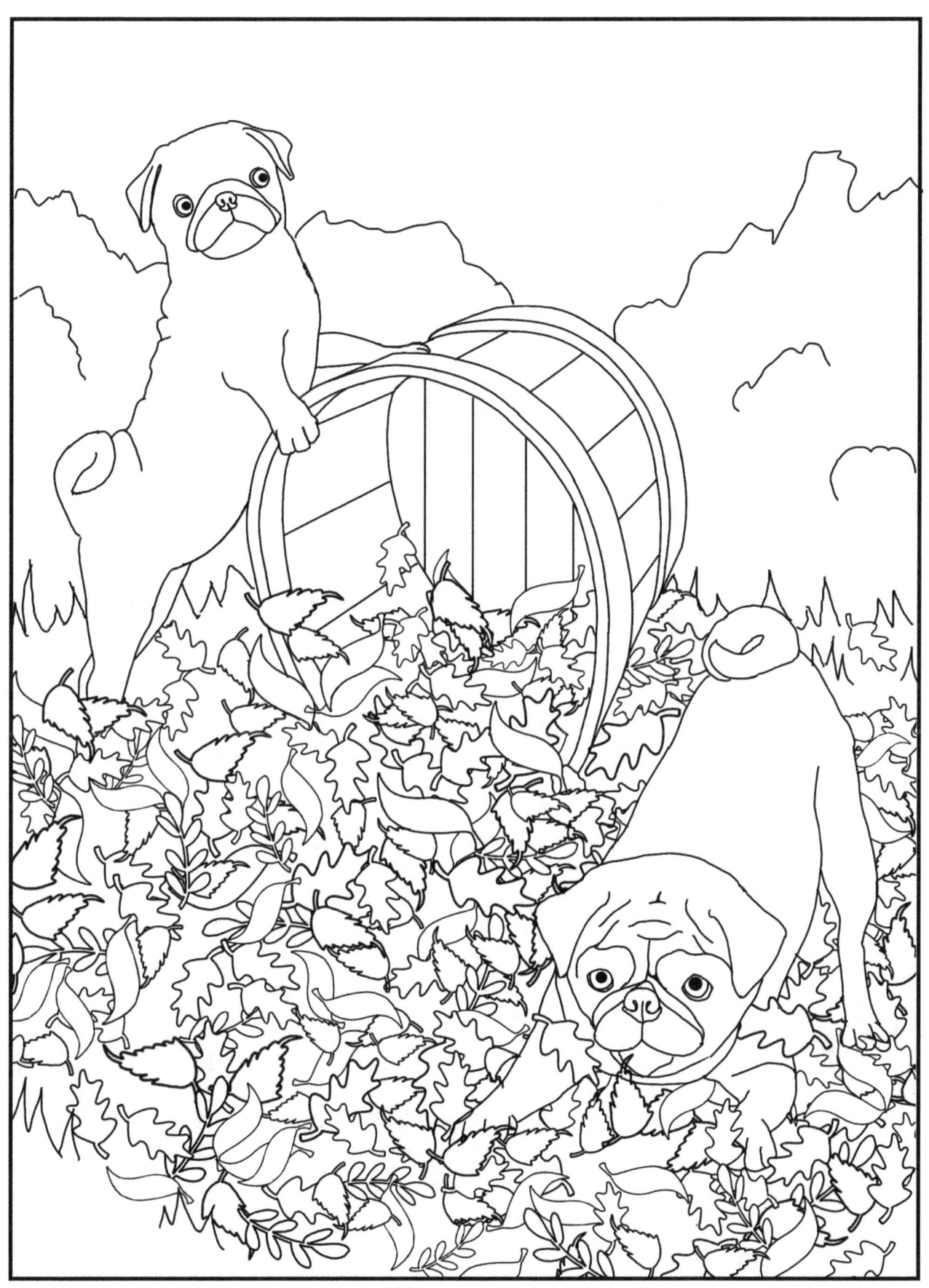

Entangled Cats and Kittens

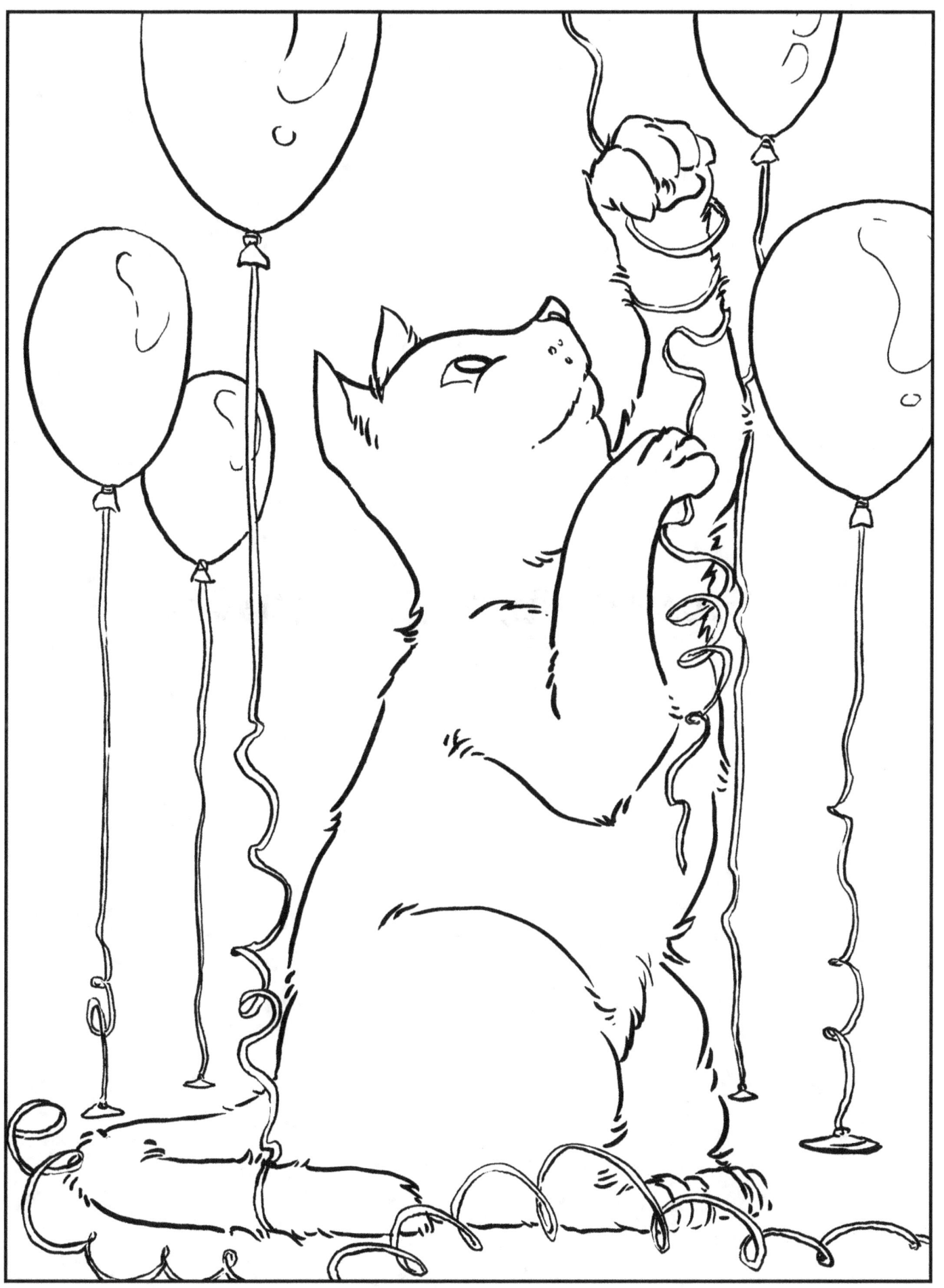

Enchanted Elephants

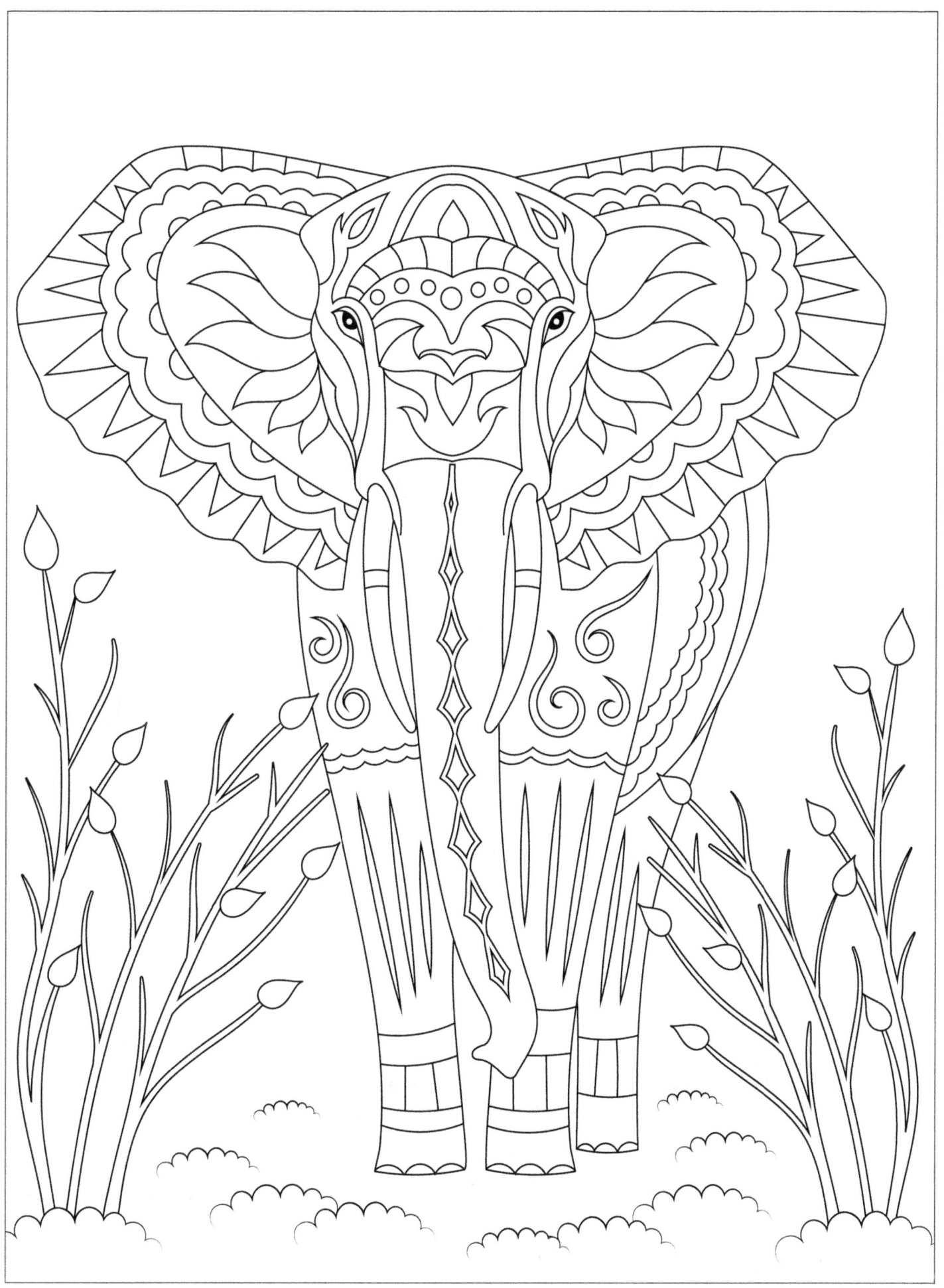

Free Bonus Stuff!

Color, cut out and share
with your friends!

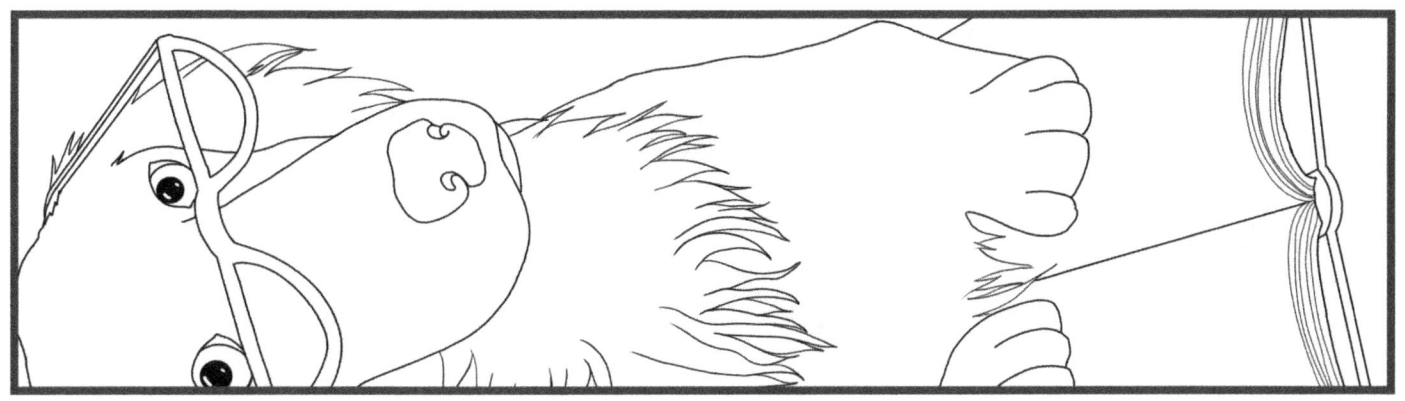

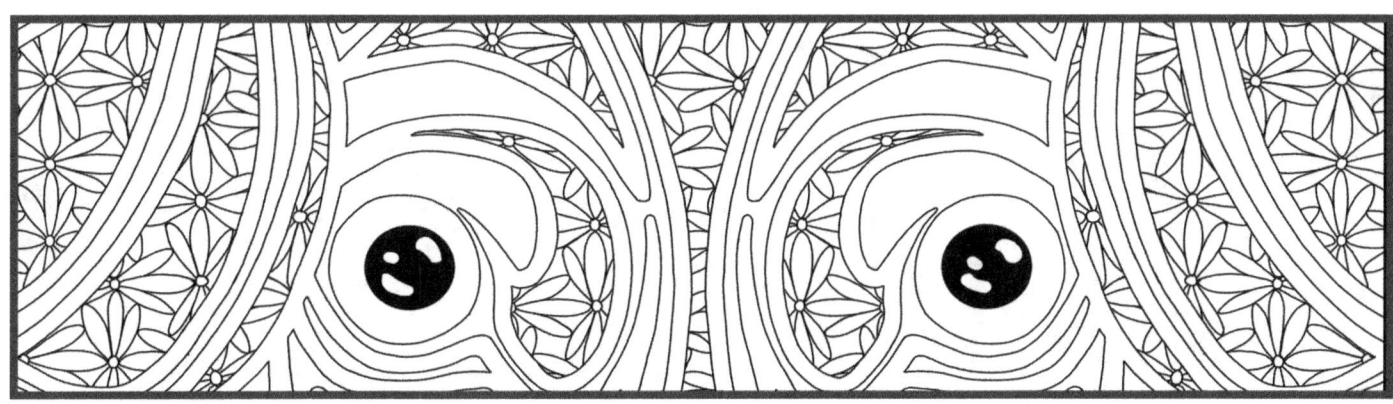

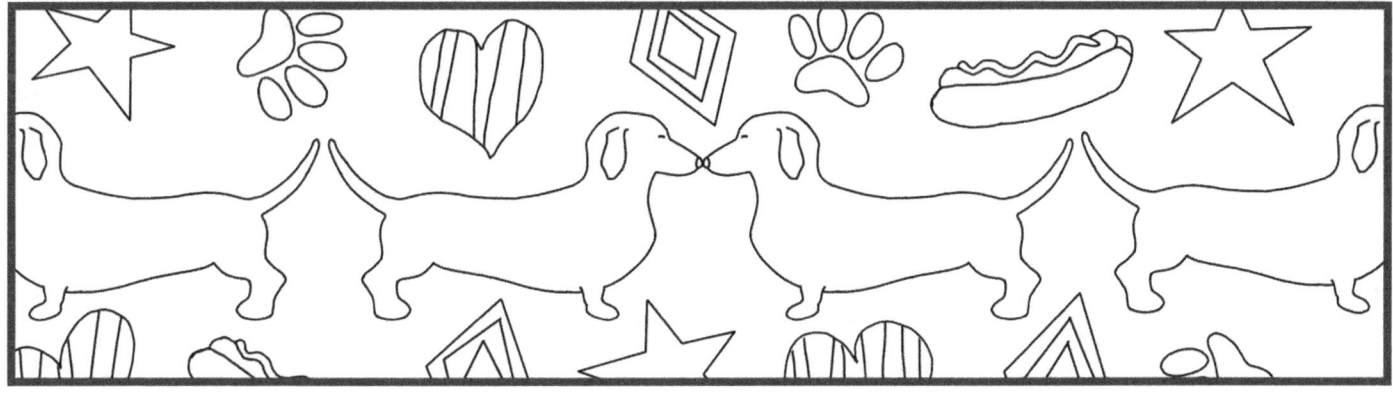

DACHSHUND